I Can Read!

My First SHARED READING

Pete the Kitty
AND THE CASE OF THE
HICCUPS

HIC!

by James Dean

HARPER

An Imprint of HarperCollinsPublishers

"Hiccup!"

Oh no!

Pete has the hiccups!

"Hiccup! Hiccup!"

How do you stop the hiccups?

Pete asks Grumpy Toad,
"How do I stop my hiccups?"

"I know!" says Grumpy Toad.
"You stand on one foot."

Pete stands on one foot.
"Hiccup!"

Pete still has the hiccups.

Pete asks Callie,

"How do I stop my hiccups?"

"I know!" says Callie.
"You stand on one foot
and hop up and down."

Pete stands on one foot.

He hops up and down.

"Hiccup! Hiccup!"
Pete still has the hiccups.

Pete asks Gus,

"How do I stop my hiccups?"

"I know!" says Gus.

14

"You stand on one foot
and hop up and down
and sing a song."

15

Pete stands on one foot.

He hops up and down.

He sings a song.

"Hiccup! Hiccup! Hiccup!"
Pete still has the hiccups.

Pete asks Bob,

"How do I stop my hiccups?"

18

"I know!" says Bob.

19

"You stand on one foot
and hop up and down
and sing a song
and rub your belly!"
says Bob.

Pete does it.

"Hiccup!"

Nothing is working!

Pete still has the hiccups.

"Go ask Mom," says Bob.

Pete asks Mom,

"How do I stop my hiccups?"

"I know!" says Mom.

"You take a deep breath."

Pete takes a deep breath.

"Hold your breath
and blow it out,"
says Mom.

26

Pete holds his breath.

Pete blows his breath out.

"That's it?" Pete asks.
"That's it!" says Mom.

Pete waits.

And he waits.

30

And he waits.

The hiccups are gone!

Moms are so smart!